Dr. Sabelo Sam Gasela Mhlanga

The Noble Wife

JUDITH GASELA MHLANGA

THE NOBLE WIFE!!

JUDITH GASELA MHLANGA

HUMBLE, LOVING, CARING & INDUSTRIOUS WIFE: AN OASIS OF GRACE

A BIOGRAPHY

DR. SABELO SAM GASELA MHLANGA

ISBN: 979-8-9899221-3-0 Paperback
ISBN: 979-8-9899221-4-7 Hardback

Assisted by: Author's Choice LLC
Printed in the United States of America

CONTENT PAGE

Chapter Five

Preface

This book reveals my heart about this noble woman, full of grace, love, and care for my family and everyone she meets. Judith is the love of my life; over the years, she has changed my life, my children's lives, and my family. She has been an inspiration to my whole family, to the church, and the community. She is a great advisor with unique discernment and skills to navigate and connect with all kinds of people regardless of their social or academic status. She is a committed Christian and she is a great teacher of both the Bible and social lessons that are relevant and that resonate with every kind of audience. She is also a motivational speaker, as well.

I, therefore, dedicate this book to my lovely and honorable wife, Judith Gasela Mhlanga, and all our children, Blessing Qhawe, Shalom Sinqobile, Prosper Thando, Emmanuel Nkosi, and Joseph Sam Nkosana. This book is also dedicated to Judith's late father, Noel Lapage Kurwaisimba, my great and loving father-in-law, Judith's late mother, Modde Jena, a humble and sweet mother, and to her stepmother, Noriah Kurwaisimba, who raised Judith from her childhood, an incredible woman, full of love and compassion. The book is also dedicated to Judith's siblings, Kennedy Kid Kurwaisimba, and Barabara Kurwaisimba, the whole Kurwaisimba and Gasela Mhlanga families who were blessed with such a formidable daughter and daughter-in-law, respectively. To God be the glory!

INTRODUCTION

This book is solely about Judith Gasela Mhlanga's life and her life journey. Judith is my beloved wife, with a humble spirit, loving, caring, industrious, and with an oasis of grace. It was through prayer and fasting for me to win the heart of this incredible woman and I had specifically, asked God to give me the wife I desired as recorded in (John 15:7). In His own time, God sent Judith to me, and I burst in exclamation like *Adama*, who said, "Bone of my bones, And flesh of my flesh... (Genesis 2:23). I felt like jumping out of my skin when I saw her beauty, elegance, intelligence, and avocado pie-shaped structure of a princess from the Amazon jungle. When I first cast my eyes on her at an evangelism crusade, in Mutare, I was paralyzed with admiration and awe, as if I had seen an angel that I imagined but had never seen before. When she was walking toward me with her cousin-sister, Margaret Kurwaisimba, she walked like a caterpillar, crossing a dusty and sandy road toward a mopane tree. I was flabbergasted! This book will reveal to you what I found and what I cherish for my entire life. Stay with me as I unpack the full package from the Lord, Jehovah Jireh, the provider!

The book will unpack the genesis of Judith Gasela Mhlanga, her childhood, her teenage experience, and her marriage to a magnificent husband. Her profession was as if it were designed for her and she became the best teacher in the class and outside the class, loved by her students and her workmates. As a calling besides her profession, she became a minister's wife, teaching Sunday school in the church to give children a sound foundation and solid ground for them based on the Word of God's moral ethics and Christian values. Judith is a woman of valor, seasoned with a godly and pleasant character. She is humble, loving, caring, and industrious, resembling a (Proverbs 31) wife to impact her community. Judith's enormous work and pleasant character vibrated and impacted me, my family, my children, the church, and the community at large.

Chapter One
The genesis of Judith and her childhood

Judith was born in the early seventies in a village called Nyanyadzi, in the southwest part of Mutare city in the eastern part of Zimbabwe. She was in the village where her mother, Modde Jena was born and lived. Her father, Noel Lapage Kurwaisimba did not marry her mother, however, he loved her daughter and did not abandon her. He supported her in every aspect and supported her well-being. He named his daughter Judith. Judith's great-grandmother, Munechi, named her, Muneyinazo. He supported her as she lived with her mother, Modde Jena, and her mother, Kuziyana. Her father provided her with clothes, milk, food, and every need a child can require. She supported and cared for her with all her emotional and moral support. Judith was very bright in complexion and beautiful, taking her genes from her father whose mother had the same light skin as Judith.

At the age of 8 years, Judith's father decided to take her to live with her at his house, in Chimanimani. It was a difficult adjustment for Judith to relocate to a new home in Chimanimani from Nyanyadzi, her mother's village. Modde Jenna, Judith's mother, had consented and agreed for Mr. Noel P. Kurwaisimba to have full custody of Judith to live with him. Judith was introduced to her stepmother, Noriah Kurwaisimba, who warmly welcomed her and treated her like her own daughter. Judith assimilated very well into the new family of her father and stepmother. Mr. Noel P. Kurwaisimba and his wife, Noriah, had a son, Kennedy Kid Kurwaisimba. Kennedy embraced Judith as a new sister when she joined the family in 1980. Mr. Noel P. Kurwaisimba was a School Principal/Headmaster at the nearby school and his wife, Mrs. Noriah Kurwaisimba, was a Registered Nurse in a nearby clinic. Judith was enrolled in her new school in the neighborhood and soon became a student at Ngangu Primary School at the age of 8 years old in her second grade, with her little brother, Kennedy.

Soon afterward, the family was joined by another daughter of Mr. Noel Kurwaisimba, named Barbara Kurwaisimba whom he had with another woman. Barbara became part of the family, too, and soon, she had a bigger sister, Judith, and a little brother, Kennedy. Mr. Noel P. Kurwaisimba with his lovely wife, Mrs. Noriah Kurwaisimba, had a complete family, two daughters and a son. They lived in harmony and the couple maintained a great functional family, sending them to school and providing them with every need the children would desire. Judith finished her early childhood in a loving and supportive family with her two siblings, surrounded by her uncles, aunts, cousins, and consanguinity on the side of her family's clan. Notable in her extended family was her grandmother, Grace Datiwa Kurwaisimba who had a striking resemblance to her, light-skinned and slender. Her grandfather, Time, was also a fascinating character with a sense of humor. I loved those senior people, who represented my grandfather, Mabutho Gasela, and MaKhwananzi Gasela, whom I never lived to see. When I was born, they were long gone, having joined Gasela Mhlanga's dynasty in the heavens. Even though Judith had relocated to her father's clan, she kept in constant contact with her mother's family, visiting them in Nyanyadzi village during the school holidays and some of them used to visit her at her new home in Chimanimani. As Judith grew in stature, and in favor with family and with God, her childhood years faded away like the mist or fog as the sun rises in the morning. Then the Teen years kicked in with a big bang, as puberty and all the pressure accompanying it shocked her and she became aware of herself, her identity, and her surroundings.

Teenager Years

As everyone transforms from childhood to teenage years, so many things start to change, the behavior, the character, the temperament, the attitude, the body, the mind, and the lifestyle. Everyone starts to learn new things. The body goes through morphosis from childhood to teenage years. One begins to change friends, begins to have new perspectives of life, begins to make choices in life, and shapes her future in a dramatic way. Judith went to middle school with high anticipation and expectations, having learned Christian values from her family from a tough and principled father. She started to implement those Christian values, and moral and social ethics that she learned from her mother's family and from her father's family, to decide and choose to please, her family and the church to which she belonged. She started participating in the church activities in her local church, United Baptist Church, in Chimanimani with other teenagers and youths. Her character was cemented in Christian values, and she joined church youths, prayer groups, and community services, and at the same time, got involved in her family chores with her siblings. Judith became active as she was engaged with the family, the church, and the community. Her father Mr. Noel P. Kurwaisimba had a farm with cattle and other businesses that kept him busy as a school Principal/Headmaster, kept the family on their toes all the time. Judith learned the virtues of hard work, resilience, community engagement, loving people, and caring for them.

As the years progressed, Judith completed her middle school and began to start her high school in a boarding school at two local boarding schools, Rusitu High School, and Mutambara High School, which she attended, one after another, respectively. Her father wanted the best for her children and empowered them with every support, buying them the school supplies they needed and encouraging them to excel in school. She expressed gratitude for attending her boarding school at Rusitu High School because she said that that is when she committed her life to Jesus Christ fully and that she was also encouraged by other Christian students at that school where there was a strong Christian group. Other former students who had graduated from the same school were at colleges and universities and they used to come back on weekends to encourage, preach, and teach the new students at the school. Judith's Christian maturity blossomed at Rusitu High School with other strong Christian friends. Judith confirms that her years at Rusitu High School were the climax of her Christian maturity and vitality. She also became a school prefect and enjoyed some privileges that came along with those school positions as prefects.

After completing her Form 4, she went to Mutambara High School to do her Advanced Level (A-Level). The A' level takes two years and Form 4, takes four years. When she got to Mutambara High School, she was already a seasoned and mature Christian. She was now able to disciple other new Christians into full disciples of Christ. She had strong Christian friends such as Grace Rwasunde and Nyasha Mutumwa.

When Judith completed her A' Level at Mutambara High School, she got a temporary teaching position at Mutambara High School and Mhakwe Primary School as she was preparing to go to Teachers College. It was during this time that she was submitting applications to do Teacher Training, particularly at Mutare Teacher College. At this time, admissions were difficult as many people applied, and the competition was tough and challenging. As a Christian, she started praying and fasting to get a place to train as a schoolteacher.

Education Years

While Judith was waiting and praying to get a place at college to train as a teacher, I was closing the net without knowing it. I was on the radar of the Lord, and he was putting the puzzle pieces together. I was in Mutare as a District Pastor, ministering to four churches, Mutare City UBC, Sakubva UBC, Dangamvura UBC, and Chikanga UBC, in Mutare. It was during this time that I was longing to have my own family in the future. I thought of getting married, but I needed a suitable partner who would complement my ministry and my life partner. Although many friends, my family, and the church members urged me to marry I was waiting for the perfect time and the soul mate. Although many people advised me to find a lady to marry, the final decision rested entirely upon me to act. I also felt a need to find a life partner. There were so many beautiful ladies in my four churches, but I had to pray and seek God's guidance for His will in the new adventure which I was about to take. There were so many voices in the air, advising, recommending, and of course, praying for their single Pastor. It was one morning during my devotions when I was reading the book of (John 15:7, NIV) that caught my attention, verse 7. It read,

"If you remain in me and my words remain you, ask whatever you wish, and it will be given to you," (John 15:7, NIV). I jumped out of my bed and wondered what it meant. I took it literally and the words sank into my core. God is our Father and my real Father. I take God's words, sometimes, I do not usually interpret verses by my thinking or my understanding, but I take them as if God speaks to me audibly. What I have discovered in my Christian walk is that every Christian has a different relationship with God and differs in some degrees and levels. No one should judge how one should speak with or to God. The way one relates to God is different for each person. How close one is to God is a matter of individuals, just like Moses and Aeron. When I read (John 15:7, NIV), I said to God that I was going to write all the qualities, the character, the type of a wife I wish to marry. I wrote ten qualities of the wife I would desire to marry. I wrote down first, the tribe, the stature, the height, the complexion, the character, good health, a committed Christian, her experience, a good cook, and the mother of my children. I wrote as specifically as I wished, and I stuck the paper on my bedroom wall. Daily, I would pray for my wife.

One day, I told my friends who were living with me in the house, saying that I had found a wife whom I was going to marry. The friends were also my church members youths, David Dozwa, Archie Dozwa, Musa, and Ngwena. My friends could not believe it, and they enquired what I meant in astonishment and perplexed. I called them to my bedroom and when they entered my bedroom, they were very alert, thinking that they would find a girl, but I showed them the ten qualities of a wife I desired, on the paper on the wall. They all exclaimed that she was exceptionally beautiful after reading the ten points. I continued to pray faithfully and hoped that one day, God would provide me with my life partner at the proper time.

At Mutare Pastors' Fraternal, we organized a crusade for the whole city to evangelize the city and we invited a guest speaker, Christopher Alams, from the Middle East. The crusade was for a week, from Monday to Saturday. We put together the teams from various churches and trained them to counsel and how we would allocate the new converts to various churches that were Bible-believing churches. We would distribute the new converts equally according to where they lived for easy access to local churches. The counseling team was responsible for the registration of new converts, allocation, and praying with them. Mutare Pastor's Fraternal was composed of various Pastors and

Pastor Victor Manhanga was the chairperson of the Pastors' Fraternal that time in 1993. The Scripture Union was also incredibly involved with the Scripture Union Director Pastor Napoleon Gomo and Pastor Ronny. The Pastors were responsible for praying for the new converts, leading them to the new churches, and counseling them. They were also responsible for leading worship and putting things in order. The members of the churches were actively involved and my youths from four United Baptist Churches were actively involved. The crusade was held at Sakubva Stadium, from 5:00 pm to 9:00 pm from Monday to Saturday.

It was on a Thursday in the middle of putting things together for the crusade when one of my youths came with her cousin-sister who had visited them. Her name was Margarete Kurwaisimba, a very devoted and active youth at Sakubva UBC which was one of the churches I was Pastoring. She introduced me to her cousin-sister, Judith Kurwaisimba. She was a beautiful girl, innocent, and kind. I was very impressed by her looks, smile, kindness, and her positive attitude towards me. I asked myself if she could be without a boyfriend, such a beautiful lady. But I quickly concluded that she could not be single because she was too beautiful to be single, I thought. Well, she was still incredibly young, about 20 years old, and not ready for marriage, I concluded. I never compared her with the on the wall of my bedroom for which I have been praying for. As time progressed, some ladies crossed my path who were almost like the ones on the paper in my bedroom, but I eliminated them one by one because they almost confused me with their characters and qualities. They did not match the ten points I had written on the paper. This is the most crucial time for a young man or a young woman who wants to get married to the right person. Do not rush to get someone who comes on the way but be prayerful, be patient, and stick to your principles and God's standard. Remember, you are choosing a life partner and if you miss the target, you will regret it for the rest of your life. Some people get married because of a mistake, sympathy, coercion, or manipulation. These types of marriages usually end in separation or divorce. You must marry someone whom you love dearly, knowing that you will spend the rest of your lives together and in eternity together.

Margaret Kurwaisimba used to live in Sakubva near one of the churches where I was a pastor. Whenever I met her, I would ask Judith how she was doing. Judith had completed her school but still she was living at home in Chimanimani and doing her temporary teaching at Mutambara Mission School. Margaret realized that I might have been interested in her cousin-sister Judith. She told her also that I was always asking about her. The United Baptist Church used to have Youth Conferences and continues the tradition even today in April of every year. All Pastors are required to attend those Youth Conferences annually, to support and to teach and to preach to the youth. I was in the Youth Conference in April 1993, and the Chimanimani District United Baptist Church Youth was their turn to serve Pastors their lunch. Judith came to serve my table and brought the plate to me. I was happy to see her, and her smile melted me. I saw her again between the services and in different sessions.

The Guest Speaker for the Youth Conference was Rev. Chigumira, a United Methodist Minister, who was preaching about living in purity, with holiness, and righteousness in honor of God. He told the youths that no matter how beautiful they may be, they had to guard themselves from being loose and getting involved in bad behaviors. He walked into the crowd, looking for someone beautiful in the crowd to give an illustration. He moved around in the crowd of hundreds of youths packed in a hall. He picked Judith in the crowd and brought her on the platform, presenting her as a good example of a beautiful girl who should refrain from doing dreadful things because she was beautiful. He said that to be beautiful does not give that person a license to be loose but that the girls should be proud of themselves and pray always to please God, not to please people. That was confirmation to me that Judith was beautiful. When the Youth Conference ended, we all parted ways going to our respective areas. Within two weeks, I received a letter from Judith although at first it got lost to our neighbor, a church member. Our friendship began slowly, and I asked her to pray for me for my life partner. She agreed and we continued to pray for each other for some time. As I continued to pray and seek God's will and guidance, one morning I went back to the paper which was stuck on the wall with the ten points for a life partner I had desired and had been praying for. When I read it closely, I realized that Judith was tallying with the ten points that I had written and it dawned on me that, "Yes" Judith was befitting the qualities I was looking for. However, she had become my prayer partner and a friend and to disclose to her that I wanted to propose to her, was exceedingly difficult. However, with a push in my heart, I finally replied to her letter which she had written to me, and it was just a general letter saying that it was good to have met and chatted with each other at the Youth Conference. I had to boldly tell her that I was in love with her and that she was the one I had been praying for. Her response was "no" and she told me that we were just friends and prayer partners. She also told me that she did not want to be married to a Pastor because the work of a Pastor's wife had a lot of demands. Those were not justifiable reasons to give me. She was testing my seriousness about my proposal as our culture demands such tests from girls to boys. Those excuses did not deter me from the pursuit of my proposal.

After such a long proposal, she finally told me that she was willing to come to Mutare, where I was, to respond to my proposal, whether positively or negatively. I got excited! She asked me where we could meet. I waited for her at Meikles Park, and we walked together to Mutare Museum, the place I knew which was incredibly beautiful with a botanical garden, beautiful flowers, and shrubs, with indigenous and exotic birds that were flying freely in the open cage that was a wide and long canopy. It was just a beautiful place to be, and I had pre-planned that we would go with Judith. We walked to the museum, my heart pumping and in great anticipation of good news. We sat at the back of the museum where flowers and birds were flying above us, swooping in from different angles as if we were on an airplane show, with different airplanes zooming in the sky. But the sound of the birds' wings flipping and whistling was sensational, punctuated by the smell of the beautiful flowers around us. For a moment, I thought I was in paradise and eternity, in human imagination but only to be reminded that I was still on earth, in juxtaposition with the one I can spend my life with and eternity. After about thirty minutes of a general talk, there was silence between us, no talking but both of our minds were wrestling to ponder whether that was the moment to tie our hearts together forever or it was the breaking of the hearts. With a deep sigh and a sincere look, I turned to Judith, face to face, eyeball to eyeball, and asked her what she thought about my proposal to marry me.

Slowly, Judith stood up, walked away from me, clutched her hands and arms in motherly fear, looked up at the sky, stood still, and looked at the birds racing above her head. I did not move, I remained seated, breathless, and knowing that it was a breaking point. I was sweating, my heart pounding, and praying that it was time. My eyes never left her, I was still looking at her with admiration and in awe of God's creation. Slowly, Judith turned around and came slowly towards me, still her hands and arms clutched in motherly fear, stood before me and shot her eyes directly into my eyes, and said, "Sam, I have been praying and thinking about your proposal. I am now convinced that God has spoken. You will be the father of my children!" I jumped and embraced her in my arms, and we stood there for a moment in silence and our hearts were uniting and making a covenant. That was the best moment of my life to have a life partner, a soulmate, the mother of my children, and a friend. I was so glad that Judith had accepted me as her husband-to-be, the father of her children. When you find what you need and what you desire, you do not wait but you move to the next stage.

I could not believe that Judith said "Yes." She was so beautiful, full of grace and elegance. Her round face and hazel eyes exhibited innocence, love, and great natural beauty I was praying for all the days of my life. Her sexy legs posture and figure were breathtaking. I stared at her for a long time and admired her beauty and pleasant character. In my heart, I thanked God for such a provision and his goodness. I had finally gone what I was praying for and now I was ready to take the next steps to fulfill my dream to make the girl of my dreams.

In August of 1994, we got engaged and it was administered by Rev. Guest Myambo, my friend. In

August of 1994, I sent my brother, Joshua Gasela, and Rev. Mike to go to Chimanimani to pay a dowry (lobola), to the parents of Judith. After paying the dowry according to our traditions her parents allowed us to go ahead and prepare for the wedding.

Chapter Two
Marriage and Family

We scheduled our wedding for December 10, 1994. The preparation of the wedding was crazy but all the four United Baptist Churches in Mutare district were actively involved in the wedding preparations. The Mutare UBC District organized and tasked each church to play its part, including Men's Fellowship, Women's Fellowship, and Youth Groups. It was so pleasant to see the four churches working together for their pastors. Mr. Jose Masango bought the three-layer cake and soft drinks in about twelve crates. Michael Myambo bought a 50 kg bag of rice, from the Grain Marketing Board where he was working. Mr. Mubare was a cameraman, Mrs. Eve Piteri prepared the high table, Mrs. Hannah Charlie provided the gown, my father-in-law and mother-in-law Mr. Noel and Mrs. Noriah Kurwaisimba supplied a beast and a bus to ferry the relatives from Rusitu and Chimanimani. All the members of the four churches contributed immensely and everything was coming together very well. I asked the Dangamvura Youth Choir to sing at the wedding, and the Sakubva Youths organized all food planning with men and women. It was so exciting to see everyone participating in our wedding.

One week before the wedding, the men and the youth organized a Bachelor's party at my house. They organized it on a Sunday knowing that I would not be home. That very Sunday, I was preaching at Dangamvura United Baptist Church as I used to rotate to preach at the four churches on Sundays. After the service, Mr. and Mrs. Ngarivhume invited me to their home for lunch. They served me a good lunch and entertained me that Sunday afternoon. Meanwhile, Mr. Ngarivhume was communicating with the elders and the youths at my house, grilling and preparing food. I did not have any idea what was happening or to think that they were preparing for a surprise Bachelor's party. I tried to tell Mr. Ngarivhume that I was about to depart. He had advised me to leave my motorbike at his home and that he would drive me home that day. I was amazed by the kind gesture that he was offering me, and I felt so special that day. They kept me in their home until around 6:00 pm and then Mr. Ngarivhume took me home in his car. He had communicated with the men and the youths to check if they were ready for me. When we arrived, there were no cars parked outside my house or around to eliminate suspicion. All the lights were switched off and when we entered, they suddenly switched on the lights and burst at once, "Bachelor's Party Brother Sam!" I was shocked and mesmerized to see men and the youths who filled my house in that manner without my knowledge. The party began. They were all laughing and lifted me in the air, tossing me around like a balloon. That was the most fun day of my life, ever. We all celebrated, speech after speech, food was plenty, and we all enjoyed it to the full. It was an impressive experience and the best Bachelor's party I have ever had.

When the day of the wedding came, it was as if the whole of Mutare had converged at our wedding. We rented the Mutare Anglican Church in Mutare City, on December 10, 1994, from 9:00 am to 5:00 pm. The ceremony and reception were conducted at the same venue at the Anglican church and the hall was on the opposite side of the church. My relatives and friends came from Bulawayo. The bridesmaids were six and six males. My best man was Letters Mukoyi, a great friend from Theological College of Zimbabwe whom we had agreed that the first one to wed, the other one would be the best man. Judith's best lady was her cousin-sister, Margaret, who had introduced me to her. Our Marriage Officer was Dr. Bishop Joshua Dhube who was the Church Chairperson of United Baptist

Church. My mother, Josephine, and my brothers, Alexander, Zenzo, and my sisters, Gladys, Mavis, Senzeni, Sithabile, Daisy, Lilian, aunt Agnes, my nieces, Cynthia Hlongwane and Petronella Ndlovu, my nephews Manndlenkosi Maseko and Nqobile Phumuzile Dube, uncles, Jonas Dzonzi, extended families, friends, classmates from Theological of College of Zimbabwe and some of my of Professors Jenny Smith and Joan Sanderson a Theological College of Zimbabwe Librarian, came to witness our wedding. The church was also packed with people from Judith's relatives from Chimanimani, Rusitu, Nyanyadzi, and of course Mutare. Mutare United Baptist Church District and local churches filled the beautiful Anglican Church. The district chairperson was Mr. Mutisi. Mr. Cephas Ngarivhume was the Master of Ceremony for our wedding.

After the ceremony, we went to Mutare Park, adjacent to Meikles Park to take wedding photos. The wedding went very well, and the food was well served, and people ate to the full and people had an enjoyable day. After the wedding, people went back to their various places. We went home and Judith's aunts had to fulfill their traditional and customary rites. We stayed two more days before we went for our honeymoon at the LaRochelle Hotel. After two days of making sure that people had left for their homes and that all was cleared, everything clean and in order, my neighbor and my friend, Machina, drove us to LaRochelle hotel, about 25 km away. On our honeymoon, we talked and planned our lives, the number of children we wanted to have, where we wanted to live, and our future, including furthering our education and careers. We spent a week on our honeymoon, and it was really rewarding, indeed. We rested, bonded, had intimacy, prayed together, cried together, and comforted each other. At the end of the honeymoon, we were ready to adventure to implement what we had planned and to follow our vision.

Professional Teacher

Judith's father, Mr. Noel Lapage Kurwaisimba, had made me sign a contract to agree to allow Judith to train as a teacher before I married her at Mutare Teacher's College. As a Headmaster/Principal, he wanted her firstborn daughter to get good careers in life to keep them living a comfortable life. As a loving husband of Judith, I assured, signed, and confirmed with my father-in-law that I would support and make sure that Judith would achieve her career aspirations. Judith wanted to be a teacher, and that's what she pursued. After our wedding on December 10, 1994, I continued to be a district pastor in Mutare while my wife and I were busy planning to both go to college and the university, respectively, at the same time. I wanted to support Judith in going to college together at the same time as we were still young, and we needed to start our lives together at the same time.

In January 1995, my wife, Judith, was admitted to Mutare Teachers College to train as a teacher. She commuted from home every day while we lived at Greenside. I used to go in the morning to drop her on my motorbike and to pick her up after school in the afternoon. I continued to Pastor the four churches, Mutare City UBC, Chikanga UBC, Sakubva UBC, and Dangamvura UBC, and the Preaching Points, small churches, which were Imbeza UBC, Burma Valley UBC, and Odzi UBC. I had also been admitted to Africa University to study Bachelor of Theology (M. Div. USA) and Education, specializing in History and Music. I started in August 1995, and it was a four-year program. Both of us were to go to school. After two months of marriage, I gave Mutare District UBC six months' notice of my study leave as I was going for further studies. The news did not go well with many people because they loved me, and I loved them. We had a good bond with the Mutare local churches and the district.

When the time came for us to both go to college/university, we had to relocate to a smaller house and change our lifestyles to suit those of students. We were now marriage partners and championed our lives together. We had to plan for our future together. I shared my vision with her, and she shared her vision with me. She got a place to train as a teacher at Mutare Teachers College and I also got admitted to Africa University. We were both boarding at our respective schools, and we met on weekends, from Fridays to Sundays. It was an easy life to be at college and university for both of us, not much spending at home. We were married for three years before we had our first child, Qhawelenkosi Blessing, because Judith was at college, and it was difficult for us to have a child while we were both at school. The other reason we did not plan to have children was that the government of Zimbabwe's education policy was that a student could not be pregnant while at college. If she did, she would automatically be expelled from college. The education policy ended in the same year when Judith completed her teacher's training in three years and then she graduated. Judith's father and her stepmother came for Judith's graduation. Judith's father was so happy that I kept my promise to allow her to go for teacher training. He shook my hand and acknowledged my commitment to supporting her daughter to complete her education. He said that he now respected me and was honored to take the hand of her daughter for marriage.

After Judith's graduation, she had taken three years at college before her graduation, and I was still at the university as my degree was for four years. I had skipped one year because my scholarship had dried up because of being the President of the Student Representative Council as the students had demonstrated to demand to get government grants just like government universities. Africa University was a private university, and the students did not qualify to apply for and receive government loans just like the other students studying in government universities and were fully funded and given allowances. Although we did not win our case that time we finally got the government loans in the years that proceeded. When Judith graduated in 1997, she was already expecting our first child. She gave birth on January 27, 1998.

It meant that she took the responsibility as a mother and as a teacher as well, at the same time. It became the order of the day for some years to have that responsibility. According to government education policy in the Ministry of Education, the newly graduated teachers were deployed in peri-urban schools or rural schools at first. Only the experienced teachers who had served several years as teachers were stationed in towns and cities. Judith was stationed in a remote area, deep down in the border between Zimbabwe and Mozambique in a school called Mutsvangwa High School. She was trained for secondary or high schools, so she was allocated a high school in the district of Chimanimani. I remained at the university campus and would go home on weekends. It became exceedingly difficult for Judith to live in the remote area alone without me. She had to find a housekeeper to look after Qhawe Blessing while she was teaching the students. Sometimes Qhawe would get sick, and she would walk long distances to the clinics or to find transport to go to the hospital in Chimanimani town or Mutare city. I could hardly help her because I was living in the city and Judith was living alone in the remote areas of Chimanimani.

After I completed my degree at Africa University, I was appointed to be a lecturer/professor at Rusitu Bible College in a mission station where there was a Bible College, High School, and a hospital. When I relocated to Rusitu College, I discussed with the Headmaster of Rusitu High School, Mr. Siwela about the possibility of my wife, Judith transferring to the mission station to teach at the mission station I was at. The headmaster was very cooperative, and Judith got transferred from Mutsvangwa High School to Rusitu High School where I was. Finally, we were living under one roof, and we began to forge our family together. It was a good community to live in, with love, care, and support. We had a school, a hospital, a church, and a college. We were actively involved in the church, community, and at our respective workplaces and we enjoyed the peaceful environment and a loving neighborhood. We lived at Rusitu Mission from 2000 to 2003, having been settled and raising our family together. We had our second daughter, Sinqobile Shalom in the year 2000 and we had our third child in 2002 when we were teaching at Rusitu Mission.

The United Baptist Church National Assembly, at the end of its deliberations and was ready to vote for the nominated candidates, learned that one of the candidates who was supposed to be voted in the position of the Vice President of the church had withdrawn his name not to be voted. The Executive National Committee decided to let the National Assembly nominate someone among the Pastors present to join other candidates. The National Assembly decided to nominate Rev. Sabelo Sam Mhlanga to join those who were contesting. I was not even there in the conference room when they nominated me. I was in my room with Rev. Austin Mabhena as we were tired, and the National Assembly conference was in its final deliberations. I was just lying on my bed when we heard a knock on the door. It was Rev. Munjuwanjuwa who was sent to call me to come and contest for the election for the position of Vice President.

Rev. Munjuwanjuwa told me that I was being called to a conference hall and he told me that the National Assembly had nominated me to contest for the position of Vice President of UBC. I was shocked to hear that. At first, I thought he was joking with me, but he was serious about the message. Everything changed suddenly. He went back and my name was already on the ballot and the members of the National Assembly were already voting for the candidates and my name was there. I sought advice from Rev. Austin Mabhena on what his thoughts were. I had no time to consult my wife as those days landlines and cell phones were not easily accessible. I was baffled and confused about what to do and what was happening. We knelt and prayed with Rev. Austin Mabhena, seeking the will of God. After a prayer, I sensed that God was calling me to a high calling to serve the church and Rev. Austin Mabhena indicated that if it was the will of God, I should take the position. I went to the conference hall and the members of the National Assembly had already started voting. The results were that the two candidates who got the most votes would be selected to be voted again, but now facing each other. In a matter of a few minutes, the final round of votes indicated that I was the winner, and I was declared the Vice President of United Baptist Church for a term of two years. I was happy to win the elections and appreciated the National Committee and the National Assembly for trusting me to serve the church with Dr. Bishop Joshua Dhube and myself as the Vice President. People congratulated me and called me the Vice Bishop of the church and very happy. God is formidable and amazing!

When the National Assembly was over and people departed, I headed to Rusitu Bible College, wondering if my wife, Judith would accept the call because we were now settled and happy with what we were doing and the people with people around us. When I arrived home and I told my wife what had transpired at the National Assembly and that I was elected as the Vice President of United Baptist Church, my wife could not accept the news. She told me that she would not leave the Rusitu community. She told me that finding a place to teach in Harare the Capital City, was impossible. She said that we were now settled in Rusitu Mission and to relocate and live separate lives again as a family was not prudent. For to find a teaching position at Rusitu High School was a hard struggle and to start another fight in Harare to find a teaching position would be a huddle. She was very correct for sure with all her justifiable reasons. However, the decision had been made and I was now the Vice President, and we were to relocate to Harare, by December 31, 2002. As we prayed together, I convinced her that it was the will of God to submit to His authority and the church's appointment.

Finally, she agreed that it was the will of God and that if God willed it to happen, He would provide the way and pave the path for her to get a teaching position in Harare. However, it needed prayer, perseverance, patience, and hope in Christ to make a way. We had three weeks to prepare to move but it meant that my wife would remain teaching for a while at Rusitu High School. I went ahead of the family to Harare to start my new job on December 30, 2003. Rev. Jealous Manyumbu was the Church Administrator, and he was responsible for arranging the housing and transportation for the transfer of the Vice President. My students were extremely disappointed to hear that I would be leaving them to go to Harare to be the Vice President. It was bittersweet for them and the whole church community at Rusitu Mission. I also felt the sadness of leaving Rusitu Mission, but I had to leave and explore what God had in store for us in Harare. On December 30, a truck came to take our furniture and I left my wife with the children as she was still teaching at Rusitu Mission School. We took every piece of furniture, but I left only a few pieces of furniture for my wife and the children to use while she was winding up her work.

On January 6, I started my new job, having been oriented and shown around and being introduced to the United Baptist Church Head Office Staff. It was the Church Chairperson Dr. Joshua Ngoweni Dhube, the Church Administrator, Rev. Jealous Manyumbu, the Bookkeeper, Tafadzwa Shumba, Head Office Secretary, Rhoda Mazemo who took over from Mai Mwanaka, who was a relative of my wife Judith and an Assistant Secretary, Angela Gororo. The Church Administrator showed me my office and the files of the Vice President of United Baptist Church. I could not settle well without my family with me. At the Head Office, we prayed for my wife, Judith, to get a position teaching in the Harare School District. During the school break, my wife and children came to join me in Harare, but my wife had not yet found a teaching position. She applied to the Ministry of Education Harare School District. When the schools opened in April 2003, my wife got a teaching position at Mufakose High School. It was a miracle to get the teaching position in Harare City so quickly. God answered our prayers, and He was, indeed, guiding our steps. My wife's worry about ever getting a teaching position in Harare had a successful conclusion. She was happy to start her job in Harare, unbelievably.

We were now living in Harare with our three children, Qhawelenkosi Blessing, Sinqobile Shalom, and Thandolwenkosi Prosper and Nkosilathi Emmanuel. I enrolled with Zimbabwe Open University, to study master's in educational administration, Policy Studies, and Planning. My wife Judith also enrolled at the University of Zimbabwe studying Bachelor of Education. We all got busy with life in Harare, the Capital City. I was studying, attending to family welfare, and the Church duties as the Vice President. Everything was going smoothly in 2003 and life was flowing smoothly. In 2003, all things seemed to indicate that we belonged to Harare, the Capital City of Zimbabwe and one would think, what were we doing at Rusitu Valley where nothing was happening compared to life in Harare? In 2003, I consolidated my position, and my relationship with the Head Office staff, and the church and applied my skills and experience in administration and church policies in my new job that I loved so much. When Rev. Jealous Manyumbu was transferred from Head Office to Glenora B United Baptist Church as a Pastor, the National Committee appointed me to be the Acting Church Administrator. I had two positions at the Head Office as the acting Church Administrator and the

Church Vice President. I started to fill the whole load of the two positions on me.

In 2004, our son, Blessing was attending a pre-school when one day, he came from school saying he had seen something that was scary at school, and that he could not exactly tell us what it was. He was behaving strangely. We tried to investigate and trace his illness but there was no concrete narrative from the teacher. This illness crushed me and my wife, emotionally. Blessing was five years old, and he became extremely sick, his health deteriorated gradually, from that time. We took him to private hospitals to be evaluated with all forms of technological equipment available. After a few weeks, Blessing developed pneumonia-like symptoms and a high fever. We got scared with my wife of his condition. I was doing evangelism outreach in Rutendo City with Rev. Pardon, the Mine Ministry Director when my wife called me and told me that our son, Blessing, was not feeling well and that he had a high body temperature. It was in the middle of the night when she called. I got up and drove back home at night, to Harare. I was incredibly sad to hear that and questioned why it had happened while I was doing God's work.

When I arrived, he was extremely sick, and we took him to the hospital, they assessed his blood to determine any infection in his blood and body. They assessed him for malaria, flu, and many tests but all the tests came out negative. They transferred him to another smaller hospital, but his temperature was always high, and they did not know what kind of infection he had. The hospital where he transferred to was having children who were dying in substantial numbers, and we decided to transfer him to another nearby hospital. We were scared for his life, and we became emotionally drained with anxiety and anxious about what would happen to him. When he got to a new hospital, they decided to take him more tests and even a brain scan. When the tests did not indicate any results of any infection, they decided to take spinal fluid samples, and lumbar puncture, which is needed to assess the fluid around the brain and spinal cord. The test was to find out if Blessing had meningitis which is a serious infection around the brain. Meningitis may be suspected in babies, but it is usually conducted in babies less than one-month-old. However, they made the test procedure on Blessing. The symptoms of meningitis include vomiting, headache, tiredness, fever, and Blessing exhibited those symptoms. After going through lumbar puncture procedures, Blessing's situation became worse. He could not walk, or speak, and his limbs were stifled. He was five years old, and he became like a two-year-old boy. He could not produce any sound, he could not crawl, or do anything. We felt helpless, hopeless, and inadequate as a Minister and a leader of about twenty thousand members Church, and I felt vulnerable as a leader. My son reversed his development from age five to a two-year-old baby again. He was diagnosed with pneumonia, called encephalitis pneumonia (inflammation of the brain) due to infection. The infection was due to infection caused by bacteria or viruses. They confessed that they had made a mistake during the procedure of taking the lumbar puncture tests that caused severe damage to his spine. My trust in doctors was dwindling. I blamed myself for not being home when my son got sick. I struggled to understand the meaning of all that. We stayed in the hospital with him for more than three weeks. I was emotionally distressed, spiritually bankrupt, and powerless as the Vice President and Church Administrator of United Baptist Church working in the Head Office.

Our son has paralyzed the whole body at our watch. During that time all our three children got the fever too, Blessing, Shalom, and Prosper. However, the other two recovered, and Blessing continued to be sick without any signs of recovery. My wife spent the nights at home with the children and I spent the nights with Blessing at the hospital. Our other children were still young, and they needed much care. We had a housekeeper called Chennai who was a significant help during the day, taking care of the children to help my wife. The sickness of my son affected me grossly and I was refusing even to eat. I was not fasting, but I was not having any appetite to eat anything. My son was only able to eat liquids like yogurt, porridge, etc. He became so skinny that you could see the ribs on his side. During the nights, I would lift him to go to the toilet/bathroom and he was not able to stand on his own or to walk. The Doctors gave up on him and said he would never recover because his brain had inflamed because of the infection. One of the doctors told us that Blessing would never walk, talk, or do anything because his brain had reversed to be that of a two-year-old boy. She said that he would never recover and that we had to take him home because there was no hope in any kind of medication that was available. That statement from one of the doctors crushed my heart and soul. She recommended that we take him to a therapist to help his limbs stretch.

One night, as I saw my son's health deteriorating and his strength gradually and slowly dissipating, I cried to the Lord bitterly beside

Blessing's bed at midnight in the Hospital and I asked God why he allowed me to be the Vice President and the Church Administrator of the denomination only to disgrace us by losing our son in His presence. I was blaming God like Adam and Eve. I cried the whole night and begged God to heal my son. After that deep and fervent prayer that night, and complaint to God, I felt God had heard my cry and I felt at peace from that time on, I knew that God would heal my son gradually because He heard my cry and my plea. I had a conviction that whatever would take place from now on then, God was present and working a miracle for my son. However, I felt I had reached the bottom pit, helpless, hopeless, vulnerable, and inadequate.

Men's fellowship (Vakweyi) was led by Dorobha, the Pastors, the women's group, Dr. Bishop Joshua

Dhube, and many others who came to comfort and pray with us. Dr. Joshua Dhube encouraged me to eat as I had refused to eat for several days, seeing my son dying in my presence. As the Vice President, one of my duties was to organize and chair the Annual Revival Meetings. I had drafted the programs and planned and prepared to go to the Annual Revival Meetings at Biriri Mission School. As the Vice Church Chairperson, it was my job description and mandate to chair the Annual Revival Meeting of more than a thousand attendees. I had organized and arranged all the necessary things with the National Committee, and we were ready to kick off. When the sickness struck my son, Qhawe, it was impossible to go, leaving my son to die with this sickness. However, I respect and honor my wife Judith, who encouraged me to go to the meeting saying that God would take care of the situation. Dr. Bishop Joshua Dhube had accepted that I should not go so that I could deal with my sick son and family. Dr. Bishop J. Dhube was incredibly supportive of his lovely wife, Mrs. Bishop Dhube. I was so grateful to be surrounded by such a loving and caring community of believers. Against all odds, I listened to my wife, Judith, and braced to go to the Annual Revival Meeting in August 2004. By faith I headed to Biriri Mission in Chimanimani, leaving my wife with an ailing son and three children with the help of the house housekeeper, Chennai, who was immensely helpful by all standards.

The Annual Revival Meeting started very well as I chaired the whole meeting and announced that my son was extremely sick to the point of death but that I had to come to fulfill my duty as the chairperson of the event, for God's sake. The members of the church prayed for my son. The Revival Meetings started on Tuesday to Sunday. On Thursday, the whole assembly prayed and some of the people fasted for Qhawe, our son, to be healed. On Friday, the following day, I called my wife to check how Qhawe was doing, and she was happy to tell me that Qhawe had started to try to speak, and he was able to say "mama." I reported to the conference and there was a thunderous praise to God from the congregants. There was a progression of his recovery. On Saturday when I called to check his condition again, my wife told me that Qhawe was able to crawl and to stand on his own and sometimes hold on to coffee tables and some chairs. We serve a miracle-working God, indeed! On Sunday, when I went back home, I found Qhawe looking alive and recovering well. Within a week, he was able to eat solid food, able to walk, and say some meaningful words. A five-year-old boy who was able to do everything like any five-year-old would do but he had taken three years steps back and now he was recovering in our very eyes while we saw him being struck by paralysis. God is a faithful and dependable God!

Qhawe, spasmodically, recovered slowly but surely. There were certain things that if one was not aware, one would be surprised how a five-year-old could behave in a certain way. Some of the teachers at schools, even though they were informed how Qhawe was affected by encephalitis pneumonia, could not understand his situation. His capabilities and abilities were affected, and he needed more time to recover slowly and a lot of support and love. Some of his decisions were, of course, not accurate. Within a year of his recovery, he was playing with other children at the Conference Center because we had moved to a missionary house adjacent to the Head Office, closer to the Conference Center. Qhawe climbed a tree and without calculating accurately his steps on top of the tree, he fell headlong, and his arm broke in half. He came home running, holding his broken arm. We should have closely monitored his play, but it was too late. My wife was at work as a teacher, and I called her and told her what had happened. I drove him to the hospital, and they had to put a cast on his arm which took a long time to heal. From that time onwards, we were monitoring his playing because he was not careful when playing. He was too adventurous and careless in many ways. However, he was a genius and a good planner. He would plan things for the following day and ask us what the plan for the following day was and what the day was would like thereafter. We used to plan things just for the sake of Qhawe. If we did not plan for the following day and the day after, he would not stop asking what we had planned. He would ask what we would be eating the following day. He would be able to plan, and he would help to accomplish the plan with us. He was such a significant help in the house. He would clean, put things in order, and make sure the house was locked and secure always. He took care of his siblings so well. He made sure they were safe, fed, and happy. He was such a blessing to us. His mother named him "Blessing" because he was a blessing to us all and the neighbors.

God consoled us with our third son, and fourth child, Nkosilathi/Emmanuel. We were so glad that God smiled on us again. We were so grateful for such a wonderful gift. My mother Josephine Nyathi Gasela visited us to see her grandchildren.

Meanwhile, I applied to study Master of Theology in America. I was granted an F-1 visa after four attempts and finally the study visa. I got a full scholarship, which included living expenses, and tuition. The PRTS bought me an air ticket to travel to the USA on January 17, 2008. I had to leave my family back home, but I needed to depart first so that they would follow me later. They could not give me and my family visas, indicating that if they did, it was unlikely that I would come back. To part with my wife, Judith, and the kids was the most painful thing I had ever experienced. I had left them in the hands of Rev. Alfred Simango, my aunt, Agnes, and other Head Office staff. The family was well cared for. I had faith and conviction that they would join me in a brief period. I knew that God would open the door for them as He had opened the door for me. I was excited to land in the USA. I started thinking back about my wife and the children. It was a big mountain to climb, and the challenge was for my wife and the children to get their visas and follow me, but I was supposed to go first before they could apply for their F-2 visas.

My wife Judith and the children went for interviews at the American embassy to get the F-2 visas to join me in the USA in February 2008. The interviews did not take exceedingly long. My wife went with the children to apply for the F-2 visas. She had instructed the children to kneel and pray when she was asked to come for the interview at the Consular window. When she was being interviewed, the children knelt and prayed. When the Consular asked her where the children were, my wife told the Consular that they were praying because they wanted to go to be with their father in America. The Consular's heart melted, seeing our three children kneeling and praying and she was moved by the children who were innocent and longing to join their father. My wife and the children were granted the F-2 visas and then Henk bought the air tickets for them. On February 25, 2008, they flew from Zimbabwe to Johannesburg, South Africa. In Johannesburg, they transitioned from Air Zimbabwe to South Africa Airways. They boarded South Africa Airways, to Dakar, Senegal then to Washington D.C. After fifteen minutes of taking off from Johannesburg, South Africa airport, the plane developed electrical faults in mid-air and there was smoke that engulfed the whole plane and the pilots announced that they were turning back to Johannesburg airport for an emergency landing.

Blessing, our first-born son, who was ten years old, encouraged his mom who had panicked and knelt and prayed for their survival, together with other passengers in the plane, fearing that the plane would crash. Prayer changes things. The plane returned and they had a rough emergency landing. Thank God, the plane did not crash, "He will not allow your foot to be moved; He who keeps you will not slumber. The Lord guards you...," (Psalm 121:3-6, NKJV). I was waiting for them in Grand Rapids Airport in Michigan when I heard that their plane had been delayed because of technical faults. My heart sank and I prayed for their safe arrival. The plane was fixed, and they boarded the same plane the following morning. They finally arrived on February 26, 2008, and I was with Henk and Margaret when we welcomed them at Grand Rapids Airport. They were all exhausted because of the long flights and the trauma they had had on the plane the previous day. It was truly a joy to see them arrive and they got the shock of their lives because Grand Rapids was carpeted with snow all over and they could not see even the houses when they landed. It was so cold -15 degrees that day. Henk and Margaret took all of us to McDonalds for lunch and my children had the first taste of one of the American's common fast foods take away. I had moved to our new house a week before they arrived to prepare for my family and to make sure that everything was in order. Henk and Margaret drove us to our new house which was well-furnished, filled the clothes and kitchen utensils, and with all kinds of food. It was like we had arrived in a strange new world where there was plenty of everything. It was a three-bedroom house, a beautiful house near Plymouth Elementary, Middle, and High School, owned by the Netherland Reformed Church and supported by the Free Reformed Church and the Seminary. It was a Christian school near our house and had all the grades.

The house was strategically positioned so that the children would walk to and from school. Henk and the Seminary had organized and arranged our house so perfectly for our arrival and for the private school for our children who were 10, 7, 5, and 3. The Seminary community and the church community were so friendly, loving, and caring that we were thrilled with the Christian environment. My wife and the children were welcomed in both churches, the Free Reformed Church and the Netherlands Reformed Church in which Dr. Joel Beeke was the Pastor with Rev. Vanderzwag was the associate, Pastor. We were so much welcomed that we felt at home, and we were so appreciative to God and the Christian community to be among them. My wife and I were shocked when we visited stores that were packed with a variety of food on the shelves compared to Zimbabwe where we left the shelves empty because they were no food at all because of the economic slump and corruption, exacerbated by commercial farms which were confiscated by the political system and the regime of President Robert Mugabe. The farm production of agricultural produce had ceased. We once joked to each other that rapture might have taken us.

We consolidated and started our new life and new home in America in a distinctive style and environment, with sincere gratitude to the entire Christian community of the church and the Seminary. The center of interest and daily routine

were the Seminary, the church, and our home. They bought us a van and I had to go for road tests to get a Michigan driver's license even though I had my Zimbabwe Driver's License. Pete Van Kempen trained and taught me how to drive on American interstate roads and the Highways and he also took me for driving lessons to be familiar with the roads and the road regulations. I appreciate Pete Van Kempen's dedication and support to help me pass my driving license which he did voluntarily and to many students at the Seminary. We told our children that we would go for a week, praying and fasting for God to provide us with a scholarship so that I could pursue my Doctorate studies to continue to stay and live in America.

We started the prayer and fasting on a Monday and because the children were going to school, they did not eat breakfast in the morning, but they would eat lunch with others at school. Judith and I would break our prayer and fasting at 6:00 pm. We started on Monday and continued on Tuesday and Wednesday, and on Thursday, Henk Klyen called me to his office, and I was wondering what had happened. When I got to his office, he had a smile on his face, and he told me not to be afraid because I was showing my facial expression that I was scared. What could have happened to me for him to call me in his office, I asked myself. Henk Klyen was the Seminary Registrar and it seemed everything was evolving around Henk Kleyn. He was the man in charge of everything. I sat on the chair with chills on my body. Henk gently said that the reason he had called me to his office was because somebody had come to his office enquiring about my plans after graduation. He then told me that there was someone who wanted to sponsor and support me to pursue my Doctorate anywhere I wanted. He said that the person wanted to cover the tuition and the living expenses for the family. However, the person did not want to be known or disclose who she was but indicated that she was from Texas. She wanted to remain anonymous. The chills I previously had in fear had changed to be the chills of joy and excitement. I teared up and became very emotional before Henk Klyen. I lifted my hands to heaven in thanksgiving in the office of Henk. That was an incredible answered prayer before even the end of the week. We serve a living God, Jehovah Jireh, the provider who remains faithful as the Psalmist alluded, "The eyes of the Lord are on the righteous, and his ears are attentive to their cry," (Psalm 34:15, NIV).

When I went home and told my wife and the children what God had done, there was excitement, happiness, joy, and jubilation in the house. The children learned a good lesson, "If you remain in me and my words remain in you, ask anything you wish, and it will be done for you," (John 15:7, NIV). It is imperative to show by example to your children what God can do for you if it is His will to be accomplished through you. Prayer and fasting work and matters, Christians should not minimize them. If Jesus Christ fasted, it means we must fast too because we are His followers. There are some Christians who minimize the power of fasting. Prayer and fasting work, especially for me and my family. We were all excited about what the Lord had done for us. We ended the fasting with the celebration of God's provision and His faithfulness. I graduated from PRTS on May 10, 2010, and we were ready to relocate to Southern Baptist Theological Seminary in Louisville, Kentucky to do my Doctorate in Educational Leadership. We moved to Louisville, Kentucky, and started another seminary life and we were living outside the campus in a townhouse. We connected with new neighbors and friends from Africa. We started a fellowship with a group of families and friends; International Christian Fellowship Ministries, a non-organization registered with the Secretary of State in Kentucky, and I was the President and a registered agent for the organization. We secured a place to lease for meetings, fellowship, prayers, preaching, and teaching. Judith connected with families and created a strong bond with the women and their children. Judith enrolled at Southern Baptist Theological Seminary to take pre-requisites for registered nursing and enrolled also in the community college. She did her work diligently and balanced her studies with taking care of the kids and the family at large.

The second Great Commission was a missionary in the USA. While I was still studying at SBTS, I had a call to plant a diverse church in America. We prayed with Judith and the children about God's direction. I wanted to plant the church in liberal states to plant the gospel in the states that needed were unreached. At the Seminary, the North American Mission Board was recruiting an advisory office that was ready to introduce and map out for those who wanted to become missionaries, to give advice, and to show them the areas where they needed missionaries the most, especially in the liberal states. I applied to several states with the help of Aaron who was at the Southern Baptist Theological Seminary in the office of North American Mission Board. It was amazing how quickly Gary Irby responded and told me that they would love me to come join them in Greater Seattle, Washington. He connected me with Natalie Hammond who was and is still the Administrator of the Northwest Baptist Convention, (NWBC). She was so kind to help me, and she sent some forms for me to fill in to see if I qualified. It was a protracted process and after submitting all the required documentation, applications, and references, the assessment team invited me with my wife, Judith, to travel to Seattle, Washington for assessments. It was a breakthrough to be invited for the assessment process by the assessment team to be considered as church planters/missionaries in the Northwest. We jetted to Seattle on April 28, 2014, with my wife Judith and Joseph for assessment. Natalie Hammond had organized the air tickets for us, booked the hotel, booked the rented car and everything was in order. The assessment began on April 29, 2014, and we spent the whole week being assessed and toured the possible areas to plant the church. We prayed about the area where God was leading us to plant a church. We had first chosen Everett City because of the Boeing company that had workers scattered in the area. However, when we toured the city of Kent, we felt that God was leading us to plant the church in Kent and at the airport.

When we received the good news that we were approved, we were so excited and got ready to relocate to Kent, Washington. Gary Irby and Natalie Hammond asked me to design the name of our church plant, the logo, the brochure, and the doctrinal and constitution of the church we were going to plant in Kent, Washington. After much prayer and consultation, we decided to call our church plant, Bread of Life International Fellowship (BOLIF). The church name became the legal name for our church even before we moved to Kent, Washington. I was still a student in 2014 at Southern Baptist Theological Seminary when we were approved to be church planters/missionaries in the Northwest. While I was busy writing my dissertation, I felt apt to pursue the missionary journey in the Northwest because I had a conviction that it was time to move on with my life journey, regardless of the circumstances drawing me back to the drawing board.

I had to seek the face of the Lord and enquired if it was God's will for me and my family to move to the Northwest, Greater Seattle in Washington. The Lord kept on confirming that it was His will. But then why was it taking so long and difficult while others it was a matter of a few months? I had to be patient and wait for God's timing, *Kairos*. Our son Joseph was loved by many children at St. Matthews Baptist Church where we were worshiping but there was one special young girl who was so kind and loving. On Wednesdays, she would take care of our son, Joseph, play with him, and change his diapers every Wednesday. This girl continued for weeks and months without flinching. One day, my wife Judith and I started discussing how formidable the young girl was at taking care of our son, Joseph. When she brought our son, Joseph after playing and caring for him during on the Wednesday Prayer Meetings, I asked her name, and we appreciated her for her care and loving heart. She told us that her name was Emma Hightower. I said to her, "We would like to meet your parents because an orange does not fall far from the orange tree." She told us that she would inform her parents the following Wednesday so that she could introduce us to them. The following Wednesday, she took Joseph and took care of him and when she brought him back to us, she took us and introduced us to her parents, Brett, and Jana Hightower, and her sister Meredith Hightower. We were thrilled to meet Brett and Jana Hightower, the parents of Emma whom they had raised to be an amazing girl who loved children of all kinds and all social classes regardless of their race or the color of their skin. We are so thankful to Brett and Jana Hightower for raising such an angel whose love permeated all people at St. Matthews Baptist Church.

We had to get to know Brett and Jana, their lovely children, Meredith, and Emma Hightower, deeply. They asked us what our plans and vision were in terms of our future. We told them that at the Northwest Baptist Convention, they would not create a position request from the North American Mission Board (NAMB) without a sending church with financial support. Brett and Jana promised that they would speak with their Pastor, Tim Harris about supporting us because their church had a vision of 2020 and of planting ten churches within ten years. We kept the communication going on with Brett and Jana Hightower and they connected us to Pastor Tim Harris. Pastor Tim Harris invited me to come to meet with him at his church, Woodburn Baptist Church in Bowling Green. Pastor Tim was thrilled to hear my vision, my dreams, and my passion. He told me that they had the money for the mission work that had been in the bank without being used for some years and that they were willing to partner with us for the mission in the Northwest. Mr. Jack Wright, at the Woodburn Baptist Church, worked together with Brett Hightower, Gary Irby, Tim Howe, Natalie Hammond, Linda Grimes, and Steve Bass from NAMB, for the budget to make sure that the project tool has been approved by NAMB and for their support.

The puzzle was coming together, and I could not believe that God was using these people to build the kingdom of God through us. Brett and Jana Hightower were at the center of it all in this puzzle. Their daughter, Emma, and Joseph, our son, connected us to be church planters/missionaries in the Northwest. It was incredible and unbelievable to see how God could use and work with the children. The Woodburn Baptist Church, in Bowling Green, invited me to come and preach on September 13, 2015, in two services, the morning service and the 11:00 am service and the Youth service. We drove with the family and spent a weekend at Brett and Jana Hightower's home. On Sunday, Woodburn Baptist Church had to hear me preach and decided to embrace us as their own. We became one big family. The Northwest Baptist Convention (NWBC), North American Mission Board (NAMB), and Woodburn Baptist Church (WBC) approved us as missionaries and church planters. We were finally approved to be church planters in Northwest, Kent City, Washington. We were so excited with my family when we received an email stating that we had been approved to be church planters/missionaries, officially, starting on June 1, 2016. Woodburn Baptist Church, Bowling Green was our sending Church. To God be the glory for using Brett and Jana, Emma and Joseph and their daughter Meredith, Pastor Tim Harris, and the whole Woodburn Baptist Church who were instrumental and used by God to extend His kingdom in the Northwest through us.

I was still authoring my dissertation when I was approved by the North American Mission Board (NAMB), Northwest Baptist Convention (NWBC), and Woodburn Baptist Church (WBC) to move to Northwest, Greater Seattle. Woodburn Baptist Church in Bowling Green, the sending church invited the whole family to come to their church to be prayed for and to have a sending-off church service. It was the most impressive sending-off service we had ever had. Natalie and Gary called me to Seattle to look for a house for the family. Natalie arranged my air flights and a hotel for me to travel to Seattle to find a house where we would be living. I jetted to Seattle, and I was given a week to find a house for the family. When I landed at Sea-Tacoma airport, I stayed in a hotel near Kent where we would be planting the church. With the help of Lorain Maddox, I signed a three-year lease with the landlord in which we agreed that there would not be any increase in the rent for three years. After signing the leasing agreement on May 30, 2016, I called my wife to start packing even before I flew back to Louisville, Kentucky. With the help of Natalie, I hired a 5-ton Auto Transport & Logistics moving truck and directed them to my home in Louisville, Kentucky. They sent the moving truck to a townhouse in Louisville, Kentucky, and my wife and the kids started packing and putting the furniture into the truck on May 31. While I flew back home, to Louisville, Kentucky, Natalie Hammond booked the air tickets for the family to fly to Seattle and then to Kent as church planters/missionaries. Children were very excited to leave Louisville, Kentucky after spending more than six years.

We bid farewell to our friends, our church, at St. Matthews Baptist Church, the Seminary, where I used to work at Oxmoor/Lincoln Company, and of course, our neighbors and my best friend Elder Keith and his wife, Dayna Brooks. We boarded the plane from O'Hare Airport, Chicago to connect to Seattle/Tacoma International Airport. We landed on June 7, 2016, and Randi Boyett picked us up with the van from the airport and we met with Gary Irby, who happened to be her father. It was all exciting and Gary Irby took us for lunch at MacDonald to treat us in style. The summer in Seattle was pleasant and gorgeous compared to Louisville, Kentucky. The landscape was breathtaking, the mountains were spectacular, and the streams of clear water undulating in the hills in the neighborhood were like the Garden of Eden described in the book of Genesis. Although there is a lot of rain in Seattle, but it brings coolness to the day, without any crazy humidity. Yes, we love Seattle, Kent, and Washington!

We started to settle down in our new home and the new City of Kent and our first Sunday service was the first Sunday of June 12, 2016. The seven of us had our first service at home and we held our first service as church planters, and we prayed for God to guide and lead us in Kent as church planters and missionaries. We were full of the zeal and enthusiasm to evangelize and spread the gospel.

I trained my family about Evangelism Explosion III, and we divided ourselves into two. Our church's name was Bread of Life International Fellowship (BOLIF). After our first Sunday service at home, we had our lunch and we headed to Kent station, downtown to start evangelism outreach for what we had come for, that is to plant the gospel and the church in the City of Kent and Greater Seattle.

Minister's Wife

As we started a new ministry as missionaries under the North America Mission Board, having formed Bread of Life International Fellowship (BOLIF), I was the Lead Pastor, and Judith was the minister's wife. Judith organized women and children as we started the ministry on June 8, 2016.

The following ministries were established:
- Fellowship - Meetings for Fellowship, Prayer, Teaching, Worship, Celebrations.
- Conferences & Seminars – Conferences and seminars for various events such as leadership, women's conferences, youth conferences, men's conferences, etc.
- Marriage and Family - Seminars for courtship, godly marriage, raising of godly children, balancing work and home, family finances, education, preparing for retirement, etc.
- Health Living- Physical exams, affordable health insurance, healthy foods and nutrition, affordable clinics and physicians, weight watch, etc.

- Biblical Counseling- Couples, youths, divorcees, depression, suicide, anxiety, pre-marital counseling, family therapy, marriages, etc.
- Children and Youth - Culture and traditions, raising godly children, choosing a life partner, parent-child relationships, self-control, etc.
- Evangelism - Campus ministry, street evangelism, crusades, training, etc.
- Sports & Games- Basketball, soccer, volleyball, table tennis, cricket, football, tennis, etc.
- Sunday School - Adult, Youth, and Children classes.
- Philanthropic Ministry - To help those who are in need such as the homeless, orphans, widows, etc.
- Translations - Interpretation and translation of different languages, e.g., French, Portuguese, Chinese, Korean, Zulu, Swahili, Spanish, Shona, Haitian, Spanish etc.

Judith organized women and they cooked for the church after services for lunches, games, game nights, singing, all-night prayers, women's conferences, and children's ministry. Judith does amazing work with the BOLIF women and those outside the church. She cooks, instructs children, fellowship with women, and encourages them to participate and be actively involved. She is a supportive wife in the ministry. She is a good advisor, and she can discern things in people which most of the time is true discernment. Judith is truly an amazing partner in the ministry, and she always brings fresh air, fresh ideas, and wonderful contributions to make the church tick. She is always honest and if she does not agree on certain things that are not aligned with God's word, the Bible, she sharply disagrees gently with you. If the church committee votes for something that she does not agree with, she can speak her mind openly without hesitation. She is a great, (*paraclete*), a great helper in the ministry. When I am stressed and frustrated with work, exhausted and depressed, and come home, she always welcomes me back with a happy smile. I am so grateful to her for what she is and what she does as a source of inspiration and encouragement in my life and family.

Chapter Three
Woman of Valor

Judith is the love of my life. The very moment I put my eyes on her, there was a chill in my spine and my heart pumped vigorously as if I had had a heart attack. My eyes could not leave her but were stuck to her as if they were glued to her. She looked so beautiful, innocent, and angelic. That was the outside appearance, but when I learned about her, I got to know who she was. I was amazed to witness her beauty inside and outside. She was unique and it is rare and unique to find someone who has both the outside beauty and the inside. Judith is a rare species, among others. I describe her as the woman of valor, the Eishet Chayil in Hebrew, which is, a hymn that sums up the book of Proverbs. It denotes a strong, industrious woman who can keep a good household, "A woman of valor who can find? For her price is far above rubies. The heart of her husband safely trusts in her, and he has no lack of gain. She does him good and not evil all the days of her life..." (Proverbs 31:10-30, NKJV). She is, indeed, a good wife, the desire of my heart.

Judith has wisdom, and discernment, is hospitable, and is kind. Our house is always full of people, the church members, and the community. People in the neighborhood love her and entrust her with their children. Sometimes, our home is like a kindergarten and the children love her too. She has a magnetic love for children and people. She does not get tired of doing good things. The poem in (Proverbs 31:10-30) points out that she is a wife of noble character, she is the crown of her husband, and that she brings him good. Judith matches the description of this noble woman of character. She is hardworking and industrial, and she is like a merchant, an enterprising person. Judith gets up early in the morning, she cooks for the family, and serves them breakfast. She always has a balanced diet dish with all nutrients and delicious food for the family. She collects and buys healthy food to serve her family and makes sure everyone in the family eats vegetables, fruits, and balanced food. Sometimes, children do not like vegetables such as broccoli, Collard greens, carrots, beans, peas, spinach, and other kinds of vegetables but Judith forces them to eat a balanced diet, by drinking water and fruit juices. She encourages the children to eat all kinds of fruits for their health. She has a vineyard at the back of the house to provide the family with fresh vegetables and fruits.

Judith always shows good judgment, and she has the spirit of discernment. Her trading is profitable, with wisdom, she is worth far more than rubies. Judith opens her arms to the poor, embraces them, and provides them with food, clothes, shelter, the social goods even to the neighbors who are in need. Judith is clothed with strength, dignity, grace, and with high respect in the family and in the community as well. She is free from anxiety and worry because she believes in God and that he is in control of her life. If she faces some challenges in life, she submits them to God in prayer (Philippians 4:6-7, NKJV). She is faithful, honest, dependable, wise, blessed, and a loving counselor to children, youth, women, and her husband, Dr. Sam Gasela. Judith radiates joy and happiness to her family and friends. She has earned the rewards. She fears the Lord with honor and humility. A virtuous wife who is capable, diligent, with wisdom, and worthy and she never fails to cooperate. Proverbs 31:23, NKJV, correlates with the character of Judith, "Her husband is a man of prominence in the community. He sits at the gates with the elders. He can devote himself to public/church affairs without worrying about conditions at home." Judith has that character, and she manages her household activities, and she can manage and balance family and her work, articulately.

Godly Character

Judith's character is pleasant and honorable in every sense. He respects herself and others, both young and old. She was raised in a respectful family, and she was taught to respect every human being regardless of their status in society. She usually says, "Humans are souls, created in the image of God." Her culture, compounded by Christian values and moral ethics, makes her stand out as a mother, aunt, sister, and wife. Judith shines and radiates love, kindness, and care for everyone that she encounters. She exhibits the fruit of the Spirit:

"But the fruit of the Spirit is love, joy, peace, longsuffering, kindness, goodness, faithfulness, gentleness, self-control. Against such, there is no law. And those *who are* Christ's have crucified the flesh with its passions and desires. If we live in the Spirit, let us also walk in the Spirit. Let us not become conceited, provoking one another, envying one another," (Galatians 5:22-26, NKJV). Judith is a genuine person with extraordinary character. Judith's house is always full of different people, including children and the youth. She is gentle with everyone, her kindness, goodness, and faithfulness make her lovable. Smith asserts, "The basic idea is that without the sharing of accurate information body cannot function,"[1] Honesty is the key in any relationship and all the institutions, including marriage institutions. Judith is always honest with everything; I can testify to that fact as the husband.

Judith's character is so extraordinary and unique, which is admirable and cherished by all those who know her. She has a big heart to forgive if one offends her in some way. "God's forgiveness reflects several decisions that we need to make to forgive our spouses: decisions to let go, to sacrifice, to trust, and to grow,"[2] God forgives, and we are to forgive. As God forgives, we are expected to forgive. So many times, I as the husband, irritate and offend her, but she quickly forgives me, and we laugh it off together. I have learned to do the same if ever she offends me. "Sometimes our marriages suffer a communication breakdown because we do not understand what is going on with our spouse. Army with faulty assumptions, we speak in a way that misses the point,"[3] Communication is the key in any relationship and more so in a marriage. Judith

[1] Winston T. Smith, *Marriage Matters*: Extraordinary Change Through Ordinary Moments, (Greensboro: New Growth Press, 2010), 96.
[2] Ibid. 163.
[3] Ibid.132.

is good at communicating any of her feelings, whether she has either good feelings or bad feelings. She is honest and genuine, which makes her stand out as a principled and honest wife. I love and respect Judith for having such a sound and godly character as my wife.

Humble

Judith is down to earth! I am so grateful to have Judith as my wife. She is very humble, and not proud. Humility is one of the characteristics of Jesus Christ our Lord. As such, as Christians, we are commanded to be humble. "Humble yourself before the Lord and he will lift you up…" (James 4:10, NKJV). Her soft and kind words to me and to anyone that she talks to, are soothing. Soft words break no bones. The humility of Judith always makes me marvel at how she does it, however, I conclude, after analyzing the word of God, intensely. "An excellent wife who can find. She is far more precious than jewels. The heart of her husband trusts in her, and he will have no lack of gain," (Proverbs 31:10-11). Humility is anchored by love and love and humility is a gift of God. Humility is the absence of pride or arrogance. I praise Judith, the woman I have known for more than thirty-two years. The woman described in Proverbs 31, does not exist in our society but portrays an ideal woman with all the good qualities by God's grace, not by works or deeds. A humble person is a person who does not believe that they are better than other people.

Judith does not have one hundred percent perfection but what she is and does, satisfies me, and I am not perfect either. However, the way she conducts herself and the humility she has, makes me admire her and magnify Christ. She fears the Lord and although she is not a superhero, she tries her best to be one. "Remember your words are not weapons, but tools to be wielded skillfully by a woman who fears the Lord,"[4] Her words always comfort me and remind me of the voice of God. Her humility and kind words turn away my anxiety and sometimes my emotional distress. "A soft answer turns away wrath, but a harsh word stirs up anger," (Proverbs 15:1). Humility calls one to be honest and to be able to be a self-controlled individual. My wife is humble by nature and selfless by God's grace.

---

[4] Selena Frederick, how a Wife Speaks: Loving your husband well through godly communication, (Washington: Lion Press, 2003), 26.

Loving & Caring

Judith is a loving and caring wife to her husband, the children, the church, and the community. She pours out her heart to love and to serve the family and maintains the relationship with God. To relate with others, my wife is a devoted Christian and loving, loves and honors God, dearly. God is her source of strength to love and care for others. Everything she does, she puts God first and her relationship with God springs forth the fountain of love. Judith reads her Bible daily and prays in her closet and with the family. She loves her children and always makes sure that the children are fed, clothed, and doing their homework. She encourages and guides those who are in colleges or universities to choose wisely their careers.

Judith humbles and submits to her husband as recorded by St. Paul, "Wives, submit to your husbands as to the Lord…" (Ephesians 5:22-25, NKJV). God has given a us model of a family, the husband as the head of the family and the wife as a helper. Paul first addresses the wife that she must submit to her husband as to the Lord. The way she must submit to God is the way she must submit to her husband. Giving all her respect and reverence to her husband as if she is giving to the Lord, is an honor to her husband. As Christ is the head of the church, so her husband is the head of the household. As the church submits to Christ, so the wife should submit to her husband. This is an appeal for personal piety in Christian households. It must be understood in the context that it is the will of God.

These forms of authority are in line with God's will to maintain order. Authority and submission are the pillars of any governing body, in the family, and the nation. Society must have an order; the household must have an order also. There is submission in Godhead. "But I want you to know that...the head of Christ is God," (I Cor.11:3). It also must be clear that submission does not imply inferiority. Christ submits to God the Father, but it does not imply that Christ is inferior to God the Father. The wife should understand that it is God's command. This submission only applies to their husbands, not other men. By submitting to the authority of her husband, she is also submitting to the authority of Christ. This is a leadership pattern. This is the role of a woman that God gave her to submit to her husband. Judith has these qualities, and she implements them, and lovingly and humbly.

Judith wakes up early in the morning to make breakfast for the family and packs lunch for me and the other children going to school or work. When I come home from work, she welcomes me with open and warm arms. Then she makes warm tea for me before we eat dinner with the whole family. She cares for each member of the family lovingly and she gives me special and loving care. I love my wife Judith with all my heart. She is the apple of my life.

Industrious

Marriage is an honorable state, (I Tim. 2:15; 4:1-4), rooted in the word of God. Judith has amazing strength. She is industrious, resilient, hardworking, and does not tire. She makes sure that the house is always clean and tidy. She keeps her kitchen speak and span, without mess. Her carpet is always shampooed and dried. Having five children, four boys, and one girl can be challenging to keep the house clean and tidy, but Judith makes sure that the children do their chores, and they keep the kitchen, lounge, and bathrooms always clean. She can stand for hours working, cleaning, cooking, and washing the utensils. I help Judith in the kitchen and the sitting room, but she does it most of the time without complaints. She wants to clean alone to her best standards. If you clean with her, she will come after your cleaning and inspect your job and she will wash the utensils again for the second time to make sure that everything is clean to her high standard. Sometimes she denies being helped because of her expectant standards.

Judith does outdoor gardening and vegetable backyard. She likes planting collard greens, cabbages, onions, tomatoes, carrots, spinach, code, pumpkin leaves, beans, and many legumes and other greens. She likes to eat green and fresh vegetables. I do not even know where she gets all the strength, balancing with her work and education as she is training to be a registered nurse. King Solomon describes an industrious wife, "She is a diligent worker, strong and industrious. She knows the value of everything she makes and works late at night. She spins her thread and weaves her clothes. She is generous to the poor and needy. She doesn't worry when it snows because her family has warm clothing," (Proverbs 31:17-21). Judith would bake bans and bread and sell them in the neighborhood when we were living in Harare, Zimbabwe at the UBC conference center. My wife, Judith is all-round talented and skilled, using her intelligence and God-given aptitude without any stress. I wish I were like my wife who has wisdom, in favor of people and with God.

Kostenberger and Jones assert, "Third, a husband was to provide his wife with food, clothing, and other necessities… Wives' roles and responsibilities toward their husbands were threefold in ancient Israel: 1). Presenting her husband with children (especially male ones); 2). Managing the household; and 3). Providing her husband with companionship,"[5] Judith has a high caliper of understanding the art of womanhood and what the Biblical mandate and roles of a wife.

[5] Andreas, Kostenberger, *God, Marriage and family*, (Illinois: Crossway Books, 2004), 41.

Chapter Four
Children Ministry

Bread of Life International Fellowship in Kent & Tacoma has strategically positioned itself to serve the church community and the cities at large. Judith is responsible for teaching Sunday School to children. The Sunday School Teacher shall be able to teach and have the qualities of an elder/overseer. He/she shall be someone who organizes teachers for each department and makes sure that all the Sunday schools run smoothly. He/she is responsible for ordering Sunday school materials for each class monitoring time and consulting the Sunday school teachers for their materials. He/she reports to the Pastor.

The term of office is annual and can continue for three years if approved by the church of which at the end of the three years, he/she is eligible to be voted in again if he is still in good standing. Judith has taken that responsibility since we began the church in 2016. She loves children and she organizes and teaches them valuable education patterning the behaviors, morals, respect, and the fear of the Lord as stipulated in (Ephesians 6:1-4).

Judith can encourage and mentor children to memorize scriptures and present them during the church Sunday services. She also coaches them to sing praises and worship songs at the church. The parents at the church appreciate the skills, talents, and passion she has with children. "Jesus did not deal with children merely on the level of what they should do or think but on the level of who they were in the eyes of God. Studying how Jesus understood children can help us to know how we should view and relate to our children and other children,"[6] Jesus gave a very good example of how children should be treated because they are worthy and should be respected by everyone, "I tell you the truth, anyone who will not receive the kingdom of God like a little child will never enter it," (Mark 10:15. NKJV). Children are innocent and ready to learn, to forgive, and to relate with anyone who shows them love and respect. Jesus taught us not to look down on children but to treat them with respect and dignity made in the image of God with incredible value. Children should be given space to thrive spiritually as well as physically. Jesus grew in a helictical manner, "And Jesus grew in wisdom and stature, and in favor with God and man," (Luke 2:52, NKJV). "By repeatedly pointing to children as models of kingdom values and attitudes, Jesus elevated those who are lowly in this world and humbled those with status, power, and position,"[7] I am very proud of my wife Judith who has a great passion to work with the children and guiding them

[6] Ibid., 112.
[7] Ibid., 115

to be responsible and respectful and dignified citizens of the kingdom of God and on earth as well.

The Biblical responsibility of the parents to the children to raise them in a Godly manner, is paramount. The children must willingly submit to the authority of their parents. Children must submit and obey their parents in the Lord because it is right. The parent-child relationship must be honored because God ordained it. They must obey the Lord whether the parents are Christians or not. Their attitude to obey their parents is in line with God's will and is like obeying the Lord. The children's obedience to their parents should be as if it is to God. The obedience to their parents should be unconditional, in all matters except if it goes contrary to God's word and according to the will of God. However, if the parents force them to sin or do things that are contrary to the will of God, they should reject and comply with the demand of God and do it. Firstly, obeying the parents is right, secondly, it is Scriptural. "Honor your father and your mother," (Exodus 20:12; Deut. 12:12). The command has some blessings that they live long in this world. Children should honor, respect, love, and care for their parents. Thirdly, their obedience to their parents will yield in that it may be well with them. The fourth benefit is that they have a full and long life. Filial obedience results in longevity. Judith teaches the children those commandments and principles to live well with their parents and other people.

Women Ministry

Judith also leads women as a minister's wife. She organizes conferences to go to meet with other women, especially, at Northwest Baptist Convention and other Southern Baptist Convention conferences and seminars for women. She also organizes women with others to go for vacations during summer breaks within Washington and other places of interest. On Saturdays, Judith meets with other church women for Bible study and to pray together for specific prayer requests. Judith is one of the leaders in the Praise and Worship team at the church. Women are particularly important in the church, and they are assigned different roles for the church to function properly. Jesus involved women in his ministry not as leaders but with specific assigned roles to augment his ministry. He valued women and they played a pivotal role in his ministry. "For Christ, women have an intrinsic value equal to that of men. Jesus said, ". . . at the beginning the Creator 'made them male and female," (Matt. 19:4; cf. Gen. 1:27). Women are created in the image of God just as men are. Like men, they have self-awareness, personal freedom, a measure of self-determination, and personal responsibility for their actions,"[8] Christ was noticeably clear and respected women in every aspect.

---

[8] https://www.crossway.org/articles/how-jesus-viewed-and-valued-women/ (Accessed January 26, 2024).

Judith as the wife of a Baptist Minister, fully understood her role and tutored other women to adhere to the Scriptures and to learn from the Scriptures. Christ respected the Jewish culture, but he went beyond it in many ways, "Even though clear role distinction is seen in Christ's choice of the apostles and in the exclusive type of work they were given to perform, no barriers need to exist between a believer and the Lord Jesus Christ, regardless of gender. Jesus demonstrated only the highest regard for women, in both his life and teaching. He recognized the intrinsic equality of people, and continually showed the worth and dignity of women as persons. Jesus valued their fellowship, prayers, service, financial support, testimony, and witness. He honored women, taught women, and ministered to women in thoughtful ways,"[9] "I commend to you our sister Phoebe, a servant of the church at Cenchreae, that you may welcome her in the Lord in a way worthy of the saints, and help her in whatever she may need from you, for she has been a patron of many and of myself as well," (Rom. 16:1-2).

The women are part of the church and part of the kingdom of God, and they have equally

[9] Ibid.

important roles in the church. "Let your adorning be the hidden person of the heart with the imperishable beauty of a gentle and quiet spirit, which in God's sight is very precious. For this is how the holy women who hoped in God used to adorn themselves, by submitting to their husbands, as Sarah obeyed Abraham, calling him lord. (1 Pet. 3:4-6). My wife, Judith is very much aware of her role as a woman, and more so as a minister's wife. "Older women likewise are to be reverent in behavior, not slanderers or slaves to much wine. They are to teach what is good, and so train the young women to love their husbands and children, to be self-controlled, pure, working at home, kind, and submissive to their husbands, that the word of God may not be reviled," (Titus 2:3-5).

Community Impact

My wife Judith is a people person. She loves people and she wants people to be happy, to eat, celebrate, and have fellowship. She does this in the church, most of the time but she wants the community to relate and have fellowships too.

Judith has been an inspiration to many people in the community, the city, and the neighborhood. She cooks and feeds all kinds of people and continues to share what she has with people through her compassion, love, and care. Some of the neighbors ask Judith to take care of their children without any charge. Some people thought our home was a kindergarten because of the number of children she has taken care of. Even some of the families request us to take in some of their youths/children to come and live with us to learn Christian values and Christian ethics.

18/08/2008 15:09

Chapter Five
Family and Children Impact

Judith influences the family to relate with other families and children to foster good rapport among the communities. As a Christian family, we have made great impacts on other families who have children in middle schools, high schools, colleges, and universities. Our children are always asked what kind of family they belong to as they demonstrate love, care, compassion, and kindness to all who encounter them. Some of our children have been invited to indulge in intoxicating substances in schools but they have vehemently, declined to be involved as Christians, respecting Christian values and honoring God, instead of their friends. Some teenagers go through a lot as they are influenced by their peers to indulge in things they don't agree with, against their faith, values, and ethical morals. However, our children have displayed resistance, resilience, and pushback on all forms of enticement by their peers. It is not true for sure to say that our children are perfect and that they are free from any delusions, however, they take their Christian values to schools, colleges, and universities. We thank God that our children still follow the discernment of the Holy Spirit to do the right things in the eyes of God although they sometimes err just like any other Christians, God's grace is sufficient to sustain them.

With social media being one of the prominent communication channels in the 21st century, our children are immersed in social media, with their freedom and free will but conducting themselves with a Christian point of view. My wife, Judith, has been instrumental in making sure that our children submit their applications for scholarships, both federal and state loans/grants on time. Judith also links with our five children to make sure that they are united and support each other in sports, finances, applications, career guidance, and prayer connections with God in everything they do and in what they anticipate achieving in their goals and visions. The children have profound respect for their loving mother, Judith. Judith grew up in a strong Christian family background and with good cultural values that she imparted to her five children. The children learned a lot from their mother, and they executed her legacy, beliefs, and faith. Judith cares for her children so much that she cannot trade them for anything in the world.

Family values always connect the family with one other, the community, society, and the nation as Paul discusses, "But the fruit of the Spirit is love, joy, peace, patience, kindness, faithfulness, gentleness, goodness, and self-control. Against such things, there is no law," (Galatians 5:22). The fruit is the result of bearing. Christ is the vine and Christians are the branches and Christians must produce the fruits and they are known as Christ's disciples by their fruits. "By their fruit, you will recognize them. Do people pick up grapes of thorn bushes, or figs from thistles?" (Matt. 7:16). The vine and the branches in John 15, illustrate that the tree produces the same fruits of the same kind. Children who come from a decent and godly family can easily be recognized where they belong. A good tree produces good fruit. Godly parenting is the foundation and the source of instilling moral and godly values in children. There are some insightful values that children learn from their parents that have a lasting impact on their lives. Children love to be touched, appropriately and meaningfully by their parents. Touch communicates deeper than words.

Negative words discourage children from sharing their views, aspirations, and visions in life. Affirmation to your children activates confidence, courage, inspiration, and aspirations to excel in their dreams and reach their God-given potential.

Parents should be actively committed to their children's homework, sports, clubs, and games. Forgiveness is pivotal in developing and cultivating a good rapport with your children. Children make mistakes all the time and parents should extend an olive branch always, not shun their children.

Forgiving and reconciling with their children after correcting them in love. Pray with your children, do Bible studies and devotions with them, and fellowship at home with their friends. Pray for their studies, life partners, their careers, and friends. Spent time with them and be involved in their activities. The family that prays together, sticks together, and achieves much more together.

The children's impact on us, Judith and I as parents has been tremendous to see our five children growing to be what they have become. God has given a model of a family, the husband as the head of the family and the wife as a helper. Paul addresses how the couple should understand their responsibility towards one another and God. In (Ephesians 5: 22-25, NKJV) he first addresses the wife that she must submit to her husband as to the Lord. The way she submits to God is the way she must submit to her husband. Giving all her respect and reverence to her husband as if she is giving to the Lord as an honor to her husband. As Christ is the head of the church, so her husband is the head of the household. As the church submits to Christ, so the wife should submit to her husband. This is an appeal for personal piety in Christian households. It must be understood in the context that it is the will of God.

These forms of authority are in line with God's will to maintain order. Authority and submission are the pillars of any governing body, in the family, and in the nation. Society must have an order; the household must have order. There is a submission in Godhead. "But I want you to know that...the head of Christ is God," (I Cor.11:3). It also must be clear that submission does not imply inferiority. Christ submits to God the Father, but it does not imply that Christ is inferior to God the Father. The wife should understand that it is God's command. This submission only applies to their husbands, not other men. By submitting to the authority of her husband, she is also submitting to the authority of Christ. This is a leadership pattern. This is the role of a woman that God gave her to submit husband. Judith has been pivotal in bringing the children closer to God. As a father, I have been alongside my wife to draw our children closer to God every day of our lives.

Husband Impact

As the husband of Judith, God has given a model of a family, the husband the head of the family and the wife as a helper. Paul addresses how the couple should understand their responsibility towards one another and God. In (Ephesians 5: 22-24, NKJV), he first addresses the wife that she must submit to her husband as to the Lord. The way she submits to God is the way she must submit to her husband. Giving all her respect and reverence to her husband as if she is giving to the Lord as an honor to her husband. As Christ is the head of the church, so her husband is the head of the household. As the church submits to Christ, so the wife should submit to her husband. This is an appeal for personal piety in Christian households. It must be understood in the context that it is the will of God. These forms of authority are in line with God's will to maintain order.

Authority and submission are the pillars of any governing body, in the family, and the nation. Society must have an order; the household must have an order. There is submission in Godhead. "But I want you to know that...the head of Christ is God," (I Cor.11:3, NKJV). It also must be clear that submission does not imply inferiority. Christ submits to God the Father, but it does not imply that Christ is inferior to God the Father. The wife should understand that it is God's command. This submission only applies to their husbands, not other men. By submitting to the authority of her husband, she is also submitting to the authority of Christ. This is a leadership pattern. This is the role of a woman that God gave her to submit to her husband. In verse 25, Paul addresses the husband. The husband is the head of the household. God's command to the husband is to love his wife, just as Christ loved the church and gave himself up to her. The type of love employed here is the Greek word, (*agape*) which means sacrificial love. Christ sacrificed his life for all believers, the church. As Christ is the head of the church, so Christ sacrificed his life for all believers, of the church, so the husband is the head of the household. Christ loves the church so dearly that he sheds his blood for the church. The husband should love and sacrifice his life for his wife. The husband is the head of the wife, and he must love her. The manifestation of his love for her is to provide for her, protect her, guide her, care for her, and provide a home for her. As Christ treats the church with respect and dignity, so does the husband treat his wife with respect and dignity. The husband must love his wife, unconditionally.

It is the Biblical responsibility of the parents
to raise their children to raise in a Godly manner and

the fear of God. The children must be willing to submit to the authority of their parents. Children must submit and obey their parents in the Lord because it is right (Ephesians 6:1..., NKJV). The parent-child relationship must be honored because God ordained it. They must obey the Lord whether their parents are Christians or not. Their attitude to obeying their parents is in line with God's will and it is like obeying the Lord. The children's obedience to their parents should be as if it is to God. The obedience to their parents should be unconditional, in all matters except if it goes contrary to God's word and against the will of God in the form of child abuse. If the parents force them to sin or do things that are contrary to the will of God, they should reject and not comply with the parent's demand. Firstly, obeying the parents is right, secondly, it is Scriptural. "Honor your father and your mother," (Exodus 20:12; Deut. 12:12). The command has some blessings that they may live long lives on earth. Children should honor, respect, love, and care for their parents. Thirdly, their obedience to their parents will yield in that it may be well with them. The fourth benefit is that they will have a full and long life. Filial obedience results in longevity.

There is a warning to the fathers in verse 4, that the fathers should not exasperate their children:

instead, they should bring them up in the training and instruction of the Lord.

This includes nagging, harassment, being harsh to them unnecessarily, and being abusive. The children are to be loved and cared for under training with discipline, admonition, rebuke, reproof, and warning but with gentleness, tender heart, loving, and humility. Children are a blessing from the Lord (Psalm127:3-5). Deuteronomy 6:4-6 is a warning against disobedience. When the Israelites would enter the Promised Land, God instructed them to be in the right moral condition and not to forget who God was, to them. God instructed Moses to tell the Israelites to be obedient to His statutes if they were to enjoy Canaan and they were to bear testimony to the truth that only God was the true God. They were to "Love the Lord your God with all your heart, and with all soul and with all your strength," (Deut. 6:5). Further, they were instructed to teach and instruct their children diligently, passionately, and carefully to be obedient too to God. They should teach, guide, and transfer the faith to their children. The commandments are to be to their hearts, both the parents and their faith to their children. The commandments are to be to their hearts, both the parents and their children. They were to impress them on their children. As the husband is the head of the family, the wife together with the husband as a team to raise the children.

The family that prays together, stays and sticks together forever. With our children, we are a formidable force to display and portray the model of a Christian family. We pray together, eat, cry, celebrate, and move forward together. Judith and I have celebrated the graduations of our children and we have seen them excelling in their education and their careers because God gives us strength and grace to move forward.

CELEBRATING 30ᵗʰ WEDDING ANNIVERSARY, 2024

Judith and I have been through thick and thin together and we have been glued together by God's grace. Our five children bring joy and peace to our lives and it is truly the testimony of God's love, grace, mercy, and His kindness to us.

To God be the Glory!!

CONCLUSION

Judith is the love of my life, the noble wife, filled with love, humility, care, compassion, industriousness, and empathy. She is the example of the epitome of a resilient, hardworking, patient, loving wife. She has defied all the odds in her journey to life. Her genesis of life, her teenage years, professional career as a teacher, compounded by her role as a minister's wife, have made Judith blossom in every area of her life. Judith, the woman of valor, compared to Proverb 31, woman, has made a profound impact on children, women, youths, and the community. Judith does not have a significant impact externally, but she had a great impact on her own family, the children, her husband, and the extended family.

As the husband and the father of Judith's five children, I am so proud to have married Judith. We have been married for thirty years now and we have gone through thick and thin together as we have been partnering in the ministry of Jesus Christ. In the thirty years of our marriage, she always gives away and she does not demand anything from me. She does not demand fancy things or money but instead, she gives away and she always wants me to be happy, respected, and honored as the king of home. With her pleasant character, she won my her as the queen of our home. She can balance work, household, her career, her education as a nurse, and the church. I thank God for my wife Judith for being my lovely wife who stands by me in everything, including our children. I wish that our daughter, Shalom, will take after her lovely mother. I hope this book will inspire so many people, especially, the wives, women, and daughters out there. "The LORD bless you and keep you; The LORD make His face shine upon you and be gracious to you; The LORD lift His countenance upon you, and give you peace," (Numbers 6:24-26, NKJV).

BIBLIOGRAPHY/REFERENCE

Frederick, Selena., *How a Wife Speaks*: Loving your husband well through godly communication, Washington: Lion Press, 2003.

Kostenberger, Andreas, *God, Marriage and family*, Illinois: Crossway Books, 2004.

Smith, Winston T., *Marriage Matters*: Extraordinary Change Through Ordinary Moments, Greensboro: New Growth Press, 2010.

https://www.crossway.org/articles/how-jesus-viewed-and-valued-women/ (Accessed January 26, 2024).